38 Ways to Entertain Your Grandparents

by Dette Hunter

art by Deirdre Betteridge

Annick Press Ltd.

Toronto ☆ New York ☆ Vancouver

Contents

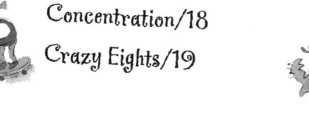

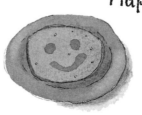

To my grandchildren, Charles, Amy and
Claire, who have never let me be even
a little bit bored—not for one minute.
          —D.H.

For the ever-entertaining
Adam, Emily, Katie, Samantha,
Jake and Ben.
          —D.B.

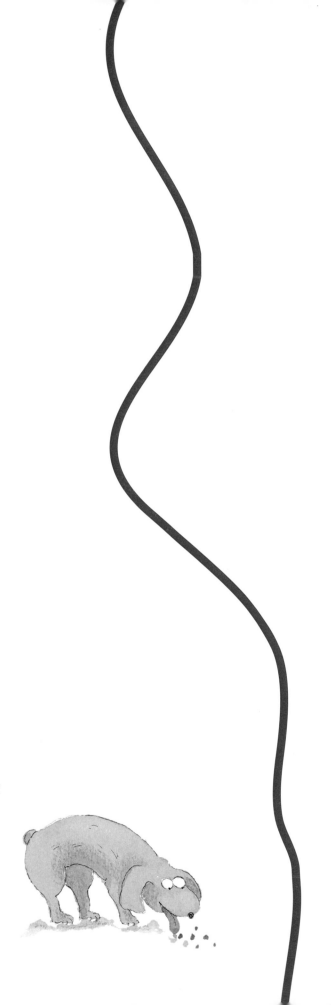

A couple of the activities in this book require the
use of an oven or electric frypan. Kids should
always carry out these activities under the
supervision of an adult.

Introduction

Thirty-eight Ways to Entertain Your Grandparents is about having fun together. First of all it's a storybook because reading a story is the best entertainment there is. But it's more than a story. In this book, when you read about Sarah and her family doing something that you think would be great to try, the instructions and recipes are right there.

You can see that this isn't an ordinary book. Then again, families aren't nearly as ordinary as they used to be either. Our lives are busier than ever before, so when we have time together things have to be special…and easy. Everything in this book is easy to make (except *maybe* Grandpa's Samurai hat!), and what you need you probably already have around the house. Most of the things in this book (and not just the grandparents) have been around for a long time, so they're time tested, easy, and adaptable.

You can approach this book pretty well any way you want. You can sit down and read it straight through as a story, if you can resist the urge to jump up in the middle and make a speedy chocolate cake or play a game of Crazy Eights. You can read it a chapter at a time each time you're together, trying each activity as you go along. Some might read the whole book and do all the activities in two days, like Sarah and her grandparents.

Most importantly, this is a book to be used. Read it. Pick out what appeals to you and give it a try. Talk about things that bring back a memory. If your rules for some of the games are a little different, or you fold a paper hat a different way, it doesn't matter. Start off doing things like Sarah's family and end up doing it your way. But most of all have fun!

Dette Hunter

I love it when my parents go away.

I thought my grandparents loved it too because it means

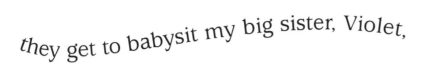

they get to babysit my big sister, Violet,

my little brother, Joe,

and me, Sarah, in the middle.

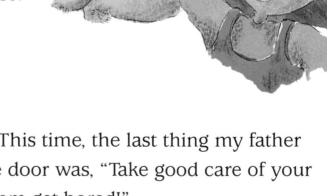

Now I'm not so sure. This time, the last thing my father said as he skipped out the door was, "Take good care of your grandparents. Don't let them get bored!"

I couldn't believe my ears. I didn't know my busy grandparents ever got bored. "Besides, how can three small children," I worried, "keep two full-grown grandparents happy for a whole weekend?"

6

I know Violet can play "Chopsticks" on the piano. Even if she plays it 20 times in a row (which I've heard her do), it's not enough to fill a whole weekend.

I can stand on my head but only for so long.

My little brother, Joe, seems to be able to entertain grown-ups just by being there. But even for Joe, being cute for two whole days is a lot to ask.

"Entertaining grandparents is easy, Sarah," said Violet. (You wouldn't believe all the stuff Violet claims to know just because she was born two years before me.) "I look forward to the challenge."

"We'd better start with looking forward to supper," I said. "Let's order a pizza."

7

All Pizza Supper

"You never order in when you entertain," said Violet, "but we can make pizza-making part of the entertaining. Grandma and Grandpa will love it."

"Making our own pizza is perfect," I agreed. (That way I can put on lots of olives and no onions.)

We lined up everything and everybody and started making pizzas.

Pita Pizza

YOU'LL NEED:
☆ 3 pitas
(each one split into 2 rounds)
☆ 1 cup (250 mL) spaghetti sauce
☆ 2 cups (500 mL) coarsely grated, partly-skimmed mozzarella cheese
☆ toppings of your choice

TOPPING OPTIONS:
☆ sliced mushrooms
(unless you're Joe)
☆ onions
☆ sliced black or green olives
☆ chopped red or green peppers
☆ pepperoni
(unless you're Grandpa)
☆ pineapple chunks or
☆ Parmesan cheese

Fancy touch:
☆ feta or goat cheese
☆ chopped fresh basil
☆ tofu or
☆ artichoke hearts

We separated each pita into two rounds and spread sauce evenly over each round.

"It's not a real 'pizza pie' unless it has lots of pepperoni," said Grandpa.

Grandma reminded him that pepperoni's not on his diet, so he added green peppers instead.

"I didn't have 'pizza pie' until I was 16 years old," he told us, "when I went to New York City to see Jackie Robinson play baseball for the Brooklyn Dodgers."

Heat oven to 425°F (220°C).

Arrange pita rounds, cut side up, on a baking sheet.

Spread sauce evenly over each one.

Sprinkle on grated cheese and other toppings and bake in oven 8–10 minutes, until the cheese is melted.

Remove carefully and let cool 2–3 minutes.

Tip: For a thicker and easier-to-hold crust don't split pitas.

Then we sprinkled on the grated cheese and other toppings in any order we liked.

Mushrooms make Joe throw up, so I made sure he didn't put any on his.

Violet's Tortilla Treats

CRUST:
YOU'LL NEED:
✬ 4 flour tortillas (medium)

Heat oven to 400°F (200°C). Prick tortillas all over with a fork and place on a baking sheet. Bake for 3-5 minutes, until crisp. Remove from oven and let cool.

TOPPING:
YOU'LL NEED:
✬ 8 oz. (250 g) cream cheese
✬ 1/2 cup (125 mL) icing sugar
✬ 1 tbsp. (15 mL) fresh orange juice

Combine until smooth. Spread evenly over the cooled tortillas, leaving a 1/2" (1.25 cm) border uncovered.

Decorate with any or all of the following: sliced strawberries, kiwis, bananas, or seedless grapes, and sprinkle with blueberries, coconut, or chocolate chips.

Slice and serve.

Grandpa really likes to talk about food, especially all the wonderful desserts his mother made.

I wasn't at all surprised when he asked, "So, Joe, what do our hosts have on the menu for dessert… homemade chocolate cake or more pizza?"

"More pizza," beamed Joe.

I guess Grandpa forgot that Joe always answers with the last choice. That's why I love to ask him, "What do you like best…ice cream or garbage?"

"That's a stupendous suggestion," said Violet. "We'll create our very own dessert pizza."

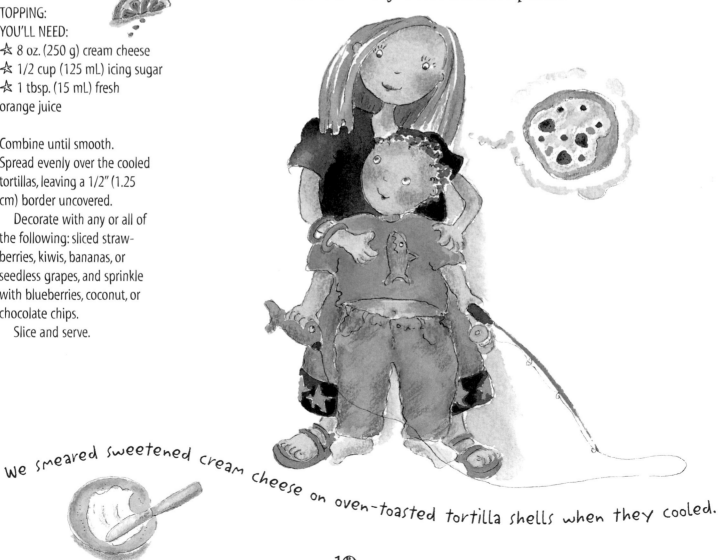

We smeared sweetened cream cheese on oven-toasted tortilla shells when they cooled.

10

Easy tip:
Buy a ready-made fruit-flavored cream cheese spread.

Fancy touch:
Melt 2 tbsp. (25 mL) fruit preserves and brush on finished pizza.

Then we decorated them with blueberries and sliced bananas, grapes, strawberries, and kiwi.

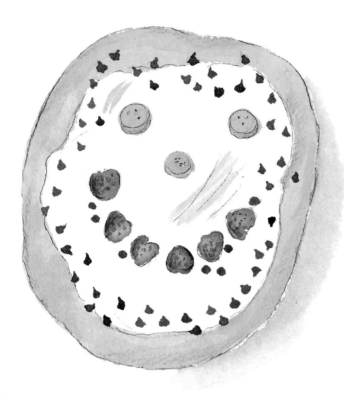

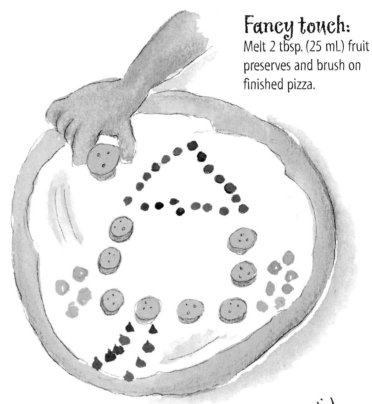

I thought it would make them more special if we added chocolate chips, so we did.

Everyone loved the two-pizza supper—especially Grandpa.

"These pita and tortilla things really are the greatest thing since sliced bread!" he said.

"What was the greatest thing before sliced bread?" I wondered.

We all helped clean up. Even Macaroni, the wonder dog, helped by eating everything Joe dropped on the floor.

11

Card Sharks

I noticed that Grandpa kept looking at his watch.

"Isn't this about the time you kids usually go to bed?" he asked.

Poor Grandpa, I think he was worried he'd have nothing to do but watch baseball on TV. He didn't have to worry.

"We're allowed to stay up later on weekends," I told him, "and I know plenty of truly awesome card games."

While I searched for a deck that still had all the cards (Joe is very good at losing them), Grandma and Joe started to make a card castle.

Playing Card Castle

YOU'LL NEED:
★ old playing cards
★ scissors

Cut card according to the pattern shown.

Hold two cards parallel to each other.

Insert the slits of the third card into the slits of the other two.

Carefully add more cards.

Easy tip:
It's easier if you start your castle on a non-skid surface like a tablecloth or rug.

They turned cards from the old decks into building blocks by cutting slits into the sides.

Violet thought we should make crowns for Grandma and Grandpa because they were the guests of honor.

Playing Card Crowns

YOU'LL NEED:
- ✯ old playing cards
- ✯ string or measuring tape
- ✯ a stapler

Use the string to measure the head.

Line up the cards (overlapping slightly) along the required length.

Staple the cards together to form a line. Then form a crown and staple it closed.

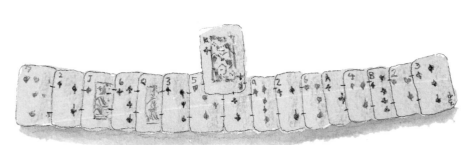

Violet stapled playing cards together until they formed a crown.

13

"I almost forgot the snacks," I announced.
"Snacks are a huge part of entertaining guests."
We helped Grandpa make a hummus dip.

Lemony Hummus Dip

YOU'LL NEED:

⋆ 2 cloves garlic (peeled and minced)

⋆ 19 oz. (540 mL) can chick peas (rinsed and drained)

⋆ 1/4 cup (50 mL) olive oil (if you don't want to use oil save 1/4 cup (50 mL) of the chick pea liquid)

⋆ 1/4 cup (50 mL) tahini or peanut butter (if you don't have tahini)

⋆ juice of two lemons

⋆ salt and pepper to taste

In a blender or food processor combine the chick peas, garlic, tahini (or peanut butter), lemon juice, salt and pepper.

Process until smooth. Add the oil (or liquid) slowly until hummus is smooth and creamy for dipping and spreading.

We handed him everything he needed and he mixed it up in the blender.

There were some pitas left over so we cut them into triangles for dipping.

14

"I don't know much about this hummus stuff,"
Grandpa said, "but I've got a humdinger of an idea for this
cucumber I found."

He hummed the scary song from "Jaws" while he
turned it into an incredible shark.

He cut a gash at one end of the cucumber for a mouth and
smaller gashes on each side for the gills.

He hollowed out an eye on each side. Then he cut a slice from
the bottom and used it for fins and a tail.

Afterwards, we sliced up the shark and spread the
cucumber slices with hummus, too.

Go Fish

Deal five cards (usually it's seven but Grandpa thinks the game goes faster if you start with five) to each player. Place the remaining cards face down in the center of the table. This is the pick-up pile.

Each player holds his cards in a fan. If a player has any pairs he lays them face up in front of him.

The first player asks any other player for cards he needs to make pairs. For example, Grandpa might say, "Violet, do you have any 9's?" (Grandpa is not allowed to ask for a card he does not have in his hand.)

Violet looks for 9's and if she has any she must give one to Grandpa.

If Grandpa gets a 9, he has a pair. He puts that pair face up on the table.

If Violet doesn't have a 9, she tells Grandpa to "Go Fish!"

Grandpa then "goes fishing". He must take a card from the pick-up pile. If he gets the card he asked for, he lays down his pair and his turn continues. If he does not get the card he asked for, his turn ends. (If the card he picked up matches a card in his hand, he can put that pair down, but his turn ends.)

Then it's the next player's turn.

When a player runs out of cards, he can take one from the pick-up pile when his turn comes.

When there are no cards left in the pick-up pile, the game ends. All players count their pairs. Whoever has the most pairs wins.

The shark made me think of "Go Fish." My mind works that way. So that was our first game.

Joe had trouble holding all the cards in his hands so we clipped his cards together with a clothespin.

"Crazy Eights" was my choice for our next game, but Violet wanted to play "Concentration."

Joe isn't very good at concentrating so I made an easy matching game for him.

Violet loves to keep score, so we did.

You can find out how to play "Concentration" and "Crazy Eights" on pages 18 and 19.

I cut some of the old cards in half. Then I mixed them up. Joe had to concentrate on matching them up instead of bugging us.

Violet cut a length of string for each of us and we had to make a knot every time we won.

17

Concentration

Shuffle the cards and spread them all out face down on a table. (For an easier game, Grandma suggests starting with ten pairs of cards instead of the whole deck.)

The first player turns any card face up and leaves it in the space where she found it. Then she turns another card face up.

If the two cards match, she gets to keep them and turn up two more cards. She can keep going as long as she turns up matching cards.

If the two cards do not make a pair, she must turn both cards face down again in the same spot.

All the players have to "concentrate" to remember where the cards are so that they can find them again. For example, Grandma turns over a 6 and a 3 and puts them face down. When Sarah's turn comes, she turns over a 6 and remembers where Grandma's 6 was. She turns it over and gets a pair.

When all the cards have been taken, each player counts her cards. Whoever has the most cards wins.

Crazy Eights

Deal five cards to each player. (Usually it's eight but Grandpa says the game goes faster when you deal five.)

Place the remaining cards face down in the middle of the table. This is the pick-up pile. Turn one card face up next to the pile. This is the throw-away pile.

The first player has to lay a card on top of the face-up card. This card has to be the same suit—for example, a heart on a heart.

If a player wants to change the suit, she can lay down a card of the same number—for example, a 9 of clubs on a 9 of hearts. The next player must now put down a card of the new suit—in this case, a club.

Eights are the crazy cards. They can be anything you want. You can put down an eight anytime. You can call it any suit you wish. It doesn't have to be the same suit as the eight.

If a player has no matching cards and no eights, she must draw from the pick-up pile until she can find one she can lay down.

If the pick-up pile runs out, shuffle the throw-away pile and turn it face down to make a new one.

The first player to lay down all her cards wins.

Just as I was starting to feel my lucky feeling, it was time for bed. Of course, Violet had the most knots in her string.

Magic and Monsters

We offered our guests hot chocolate, but Grandma said, "I hardly sleep a wink as it is and I'm afraid chocolate will keep me awake."

So we all had a maple syrup magic potion instead.

Maple Syrup Magic Potion

Fill each mug with about
☆ 1 cup (250 mL) milk
☆ Stir in 1 tbsp. (15 mL) real maple syrup

Microwave on high about 60 seconds or until warm.

We stirred maple syrup into each cup of milk and heated it in the microwave.

"A soothing soporific," Violet pronounced.
Grandma agreed.

"I hope my shark doesn't give us nightmares," said Grandpa.

The mention of nightmares reminded me that we should give the scary spaces under the beds a good dose of our special monster spray. I knew that Grandma and Grandpa would sleep a lot better knowing that all the night noises were under control.

Monster Spray

✿ Add a few drops of perfume and/or aftershave to a spray bottle of water.

Grandma let us add some of her perfume to our monster spray to make it extra powerful.

By the time we had done every bedtime thing we usually do with Mom and Dad (and maybe a few more), Grandpa and Grandma were ready for bed too.

Morning Smiles

Grandparents get up much earlier on Saturday morning than parents, so we had to start our entertaining early.

"You always put your guests first," announced Violet as she turned off the cartoons. We made an amazing juice for the occasion.

I named our special sparkly drink "the goldfish."

The Goldfish

✻ Add 1 cup (250 mL) club soda or carbonated bottled water to
✻ 3 cups (750 mL) orange juice.
Stir.

Easy tip:
If you don't happen to have a slippery slice of mango, a thin slice of lemon or orange works as a credible fish.

We mixed bubbly bottled water into boring old orange juice. I thought it would look more like a real goldfish if we used only soda water, but Violet said you have to have orange juice for breakfast.

We put a slippery slice of mango in a plastic lunch bag and poured in some juice. Then we put in a straw and tightly closed it with a twist tie.

I know Grandma and Grandpa usually have oatmeal. However, any way you cook it, oatmeal isn't all that much fun. Pancakes are definitely fun.

We needed a syrup for the pancakes. Grandma says she has a sweet tooth, so we invented the sweetest, slipperiest, stickiest syrup we could. Sweet enough for all her teeth!

Sweet-tooth Syrup

YOU'LL NEED:
* ✬ 1/2 cup (125 mL) brown sugar
* ✬ 1 tbsp. (15 mL) flour
* ✬ 1 tsp. (5 mL) cinnamon
* ✬ 1-1/2 cups (375 mL) orange juice
* ✬ 2 tsp. (10 mL) butter or margarine

Mix brown sugar, flour, and cinnamon in a small saucepan.
    Add orange juice and butter and heat over med/high heat until syrup thickens.
    Stir constantly.

We asked Grandma to stir it until it was thick and bubbly.

I asked Grandpa, "Do you know why pancakes are like baseball games?"
"I can't imagine," teased Grandpa. "I haven't seen a baseball game lately."
"Because they both need a batter!" I said.

Grandma set the electric frypan on the table so it was easy for us to see. "Keep a close eye on Joe," she said. "That pan is hot."

I kept two close eyes on him because I know a quick trip to the emergency room is not what Dad meant by "not letting them get bored."

We told Grandma a really neat way to make pancake letters so we could eat our words!

Eat-your-words Pancakes

YOU'LL NEED:
- ☆ 1-1/2 cups (375 mL) all-purpose flour
- ☆ 1 tbsp. (15 mL) baking powder
- ☆ 1 tbsp. (15 mL) granulated sugar
- ☆ 1/2 tsp. (2 mL) salt
- ☆ 1 egg
- ☆ 1-3/4 cups (425 mL) milk
- ☆ 2 tbsp. (25 mL) vegetable oil

Preheat electric frypan (griddle or skillet) to 375°F (190°C) degrees.

In a large bowl, combine flour, baking powder, sugar, and salt. Stir.

In a small bowl, beat together egg, milk, and oil. Add all at once to the dry ingredients. Beat together until almost smooth.

Pour batter into the squeeze bottle.

Tip:

Snip off the tip of the condiment container for a larger opening.

First, we made pancake batter and poured it into a plastic condiment dispenser

and Grandma squeezed the batter onto the frypan in the shape of letters.

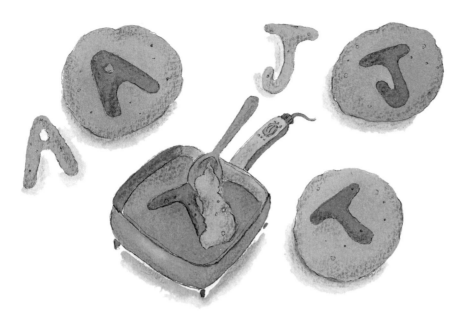

Grease frypan. Squeeze batter onto the frypan in the shape of a letter. Repeat until the skillet is full of letter-pancakes.

When bubbles appear on the top of the pancakes, turn them with a spatula. Cook for about 30 more seconds or until golden.

Tip: You can drizzle batter onto the frypan from the tip of a spoon. It's just not as neat.

She turned some letters into personalized pancakes for each of us.

Personalized Pancakes

Squeeze the batter onto the frypan in the reverse shape of the desired initial.

Give the letter a few seconds to brown, then thinly spoon the batter for the pancake overtop. When bubbles appear, turn and complete cooking. (Makes an alphabet of letters.)

Tip: If you need to thin the batter, add milk a little at a time.

Since Joe doesn't know many letters we asked her to make a happy face pancake for him.

Happy Face Pancake

These are easier than Personalized Pancakes. Instead of a letter, squeeze dots of batter forming eyes and a strip of batter for a smile onto the frypan.

Creative crayoning

After breakfast we brought out our big box of crayons and a whole pile of paper. Grandma started right in drawing.

"I can still remember the wonderful smell of my first box of crayons," she sighed, as she drew a little house with a sun and a cloud.

"Oh, Grandma," I said, "you need to loosen up a little."

I put on my favorite CD and we drew to the music.

I showed her how she could tape two crayons together and make great loopy loops.

Or make wonderful swirls with the flat side of a peeled crayon.

Joe turned his into caterpillars and snakes.

When the music got faster we all scribbled. (Joe was very good at that.)
Afterwards, we looked at all the scribbles and turned them into crazy creatures.

"I think I'll try to catch the score of last night's ballgame," said Grandpa "I was never much of an artist, anyway."
"You never know until you try," said Violet.

Grandpa and Violet made really cool rubbings of the coins and keys from Grandpa's pocket.

Easy Rubbings

Use any firm, textured objects, such as coins, keys, leaves, or patterned surfaces.

Place the object under a piece of thin paper.

With a pencil or crayon, "rub" the surface of the object through the paper. You will see your copy of the object—the rubbing—appear immediately.

We all tried rubbing on whatever we could find—leaves, paper clips, and even fabric.

Before long Joe was sticking crayons in his hair and turning himself into an alien. (Some of his cuteness was definitely starting to wear thin.) I was afraid that Grandpa was looking a little bored, too. It was time for a time-out.

Grandpa has been taking walks for so long, I think he's forgotten how interesting they can be. Joe is so close to the ground he can find all kinds of cool (and some not so cool) things.

I found binoculars for Grandpa, and I made Joe a set of bird-watching binoculars by wrapping two paper rolls together with masking tape.

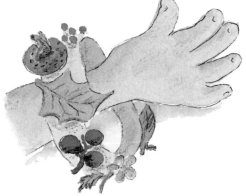

I wrapped a wide strip of masking tape (sticky side out) on Joe's wrist so he could stick on some of the treasures he found on the walk.

he Gala Luncheon

We were really getting to be excellent entertainers. I think Grandma was impressed. She offered to help us plan a special lunch.

"A gala luncheon," said Violet, "with place mats, napkin rings, and even name cards."

I found almost everything we needed in the recycle box.

Violet wanted to make the place mats. She is very good at cutting straight.

Place Mats

YOU'LL NEED:
- ✯ scrap paper and magazines
- ✯ scissors
- ✯ glue

Fold a piece of paper in half so that the short sides are together.

Start cutting at the folded edge. Make sure that the cuts (about 7 in all) stop about 1"(2.5 cm) from the open edge.

Unfold the paper and you have a paper loom.

Cut or tear strips of colored paper or magazine. Make sure that they are as long as the width of your loom.

Start with the first slit in your loom and weave a strip of paper over and under, then over, until the strip is woven into the loom.

Use a second strip and do the same thing. This time make sure that the over-and-under pattern is opposite to the first strip. Keep weaving strips into the slits until you run out of room.

If you like, put a dot of glue on the end of each strip when you are finished, to keep the strips from working loose.

She made a paper loom by folding a sheet of paper in half and making cuts into the folded edge.

Then she cut strips of magazine and wove them into the paper loom.

Grandma and I made the napkin holders.

Grandma cut a paper tube into 2" (5 cm) circles. I made amazing designs on each with markers.

We also tried wrapping the tubes with yarn for "a very professional look."

Since Violet was still weaving place mats, Grandma and I practiced fancy napkin folding. (With Joe around you can never have too many napkins.)

We made accordion pleats in paper napkins and put them in our holders.

I thought we could get along without place cards, since we all knew where we were supposed to sit. But Violet insisted.

Pop-up Place Cards

YOU'LL NEED:
☆ heavy paper or cardboard, about 4" by 6" (10 cm by 15 cm)
☆ scissors and markers

Fold the paper lengthwise. Unfold and write the person's name along the folded edge.

Draw around the name with a thick marker as shown. Poke the tip of your scissors in and cut along the top line. Be sure to leave both ends of the fold line attached.

Bend the card back along the fold and the name pops up.

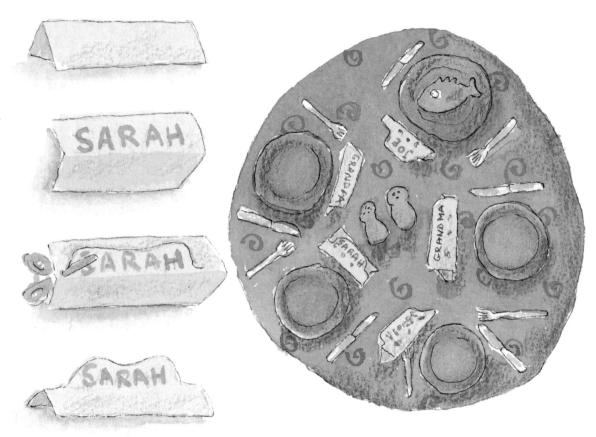

Grandma and I made place cards for everyone and decorated them with funny fingerprint people and animals.

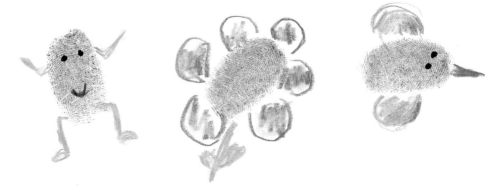

We pressed our fingers on a stamp pad, then onto the place card. We turned our prints into anything we felt like.

"Belly Button soup would be an excellent entrée for our gala meal," decided Violet.

"Belly Button soup!!" exclaimed Grandma. "You know, when I was a girl, no one even mentioned belly buttons. Now they seem to be popping up everywhere, even in soup."

"Oh, Grandma," I laughed, "they're not real belly buttons. They're made of tortellini pasta."

After the washing, peeling, slicing, simmering, and chopping, we plopped the belly buttons into the stock and soon it was soup.

Belly Button Soup

YOU'LL NEED:
- 2 tbsp. (25 mL) olive oil
- 1 clove garlic, minced
- 1 onion, finely chopped
- 1 cup (250 mL) chopped cabbage
- 1 medium carrot, chopped
- 1 handful of green beans cut in thirds
- 1 zucchini cut in rounds (substitute or add any vegetables you want)
- pinch of cayenne (optional)
- 6 cups (1.5 L) beef or vegetable stock
- 8 oz. (250 g) fresh tortellini
- grated Parmesan cheese
- finely chopped parsley and basil (optional)

Fry garlic and onion in olive oil 'til soft over medium/high heat. Add cabbage, carrot, zucchini, green beans...or frozen corn or peas, tomatoes, broccoli. Cook 5 minutes.

Add vegetable mixture to stock. Bring to a boil and simmer 30 minutes. Add "belly buttons" and cook until tender...about 8 minutes.

Serve piping hot with lots of grated Parmesan cheese on top. Sprinkle with parsley and basil.

Grandpa's Chocolate Cake

YOU'LL NEED:
DRY INGREDIENTS:
☆ 2-1/2 cups (625 mL) flour
☆ 1-1/2 cups (375 mL) sugar
☆ 6 tbsp. (90 mL) unsweetened cocoa powder
☆ 2 tsp. (10 mL) baking soda
☆ I tsp. (5 mL) salt

Measure all the dry ingredients into a 9"x12" (24x30 cm) pan.

Stir with a fork until well mixed. Make a hole in the center of the dry ingredients and add the following liquid ingredients.

LIQUID INGREDIENTS:
☆ 1/2 cup (125 mL) vegetable oil
☆ 2 tsp. (10 mL) vanilla
☆ 2 tbsp. (25 mL) vinegar
☆ 2 cups (500 mL) cold water

Mix thoroughly with a fork until all the dry ingredients are moistened.

Bake at 350°F (180°C) for 30 minutes or until a toothpick inserted in the center comes out clean.

"Nothing beats the aroma of bubbling broth!" boomed Grandpa. "It reminds me of my mother's kitchen, only she would have whipped up a chocolate cake as well! It's too bad men weren't allowed in the kitchen in those days or I'd know how to make one for you now."

"It's never too late to learn," said Violet, as she led him to the counter. "This cake is as easy as pie and you only have to wash one pan!"

Violet helped Grandpa measure all the dry ingredients.
Then they made a big hole in the middle and dumped in all the wet ingredients.
They stirred that with a fork and popped it in the oven.

When the cake was baking, Grandpa said, "It's not chocolate cake without chocolate frosting."

This time Grandma didn't remind him about his diet.

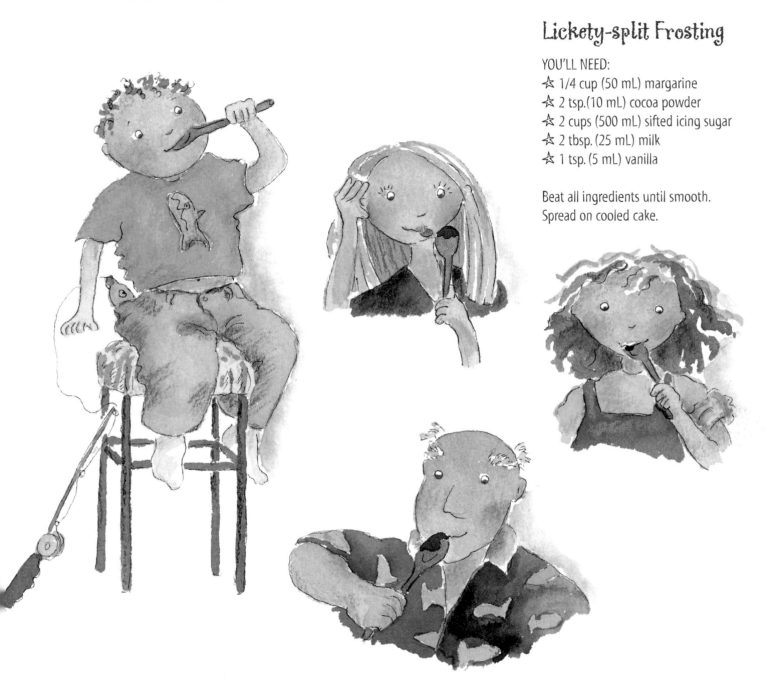

Lickety-split Frosting

YOU'LL NEED:
- ⭐ 1/4 cup (50 mL) margarine
- ⭐ 2 tsp. (10 mL) cocoa powder
- ⭐ 2 cups (500 mL) sifted icing sugar
- ⭐ 2 tbsp. (25 mL) milk
- ⭐ 1 tsp. (5 mL) vanilla

Beat all ingredients until smooth. Spread on cooled cake.

We all took turns stirring, so we each had a spoon to lick.

We decided that Macaroni needed a treat too. We were making everything "from scratch," as Grandma called it, and Macaroni knows more than anyone about scratching.

Macaroni will eat anything, no matter how it tastes, so we let Joe make the dog biscuits.

Mac's Microwave Munchies

✵ 2 cups (500 mL) flour (Mac likes whole wheat but any kind is fine)
✵ 1/4 cup (50 mL) large-flake oatmeal
✵ 1 egg
✵ 1 tsp. (5 mL) garlic powder (if your dog likes garlic)
✵ 2 tsp. (10 mL) instant beef stock mix
✵ 2/3 cup (150 mL) hot water

Place flour in a bowl, add other ingredients, and mix well.

Shape dough into a ball and roll out on a lightly floured surface to 1" (about 2.5 cm) thick.

Cut with cookie cutters (we have a dog-bone shaped one.) Re-roll any leftover dough and repeat. Arrange four at a time on a shallow baking dish or Pyrex pie plate.

Microwave on high for 3 minutes. Turn over and cook for 2 more minutes. Let cool until hardened.

They rolled out the dough and Joe cut it into dog biscuits. He arranged them on the plate, and Grandma microwaved them.

Easy-peasy Puppets

Joe wanted to watch TV while we waited for the lunch to cook.

"I never even had TV when I was Joe's age," said Grandma, "but I loved the puppet shows at the library. If I were a crafty kind of grandmother, I'd make a puppet for Joe right now."

"Joe is very happy when I just put a plain old sock on my hand and make it talk," I told her. "In two minutes I can show you how to make wonderful puppets."

"Great!" said Grandma.

I drew on my fingers with washable colored markers for the easiest puppets ever.

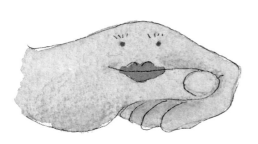

And then on my hand.

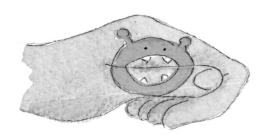

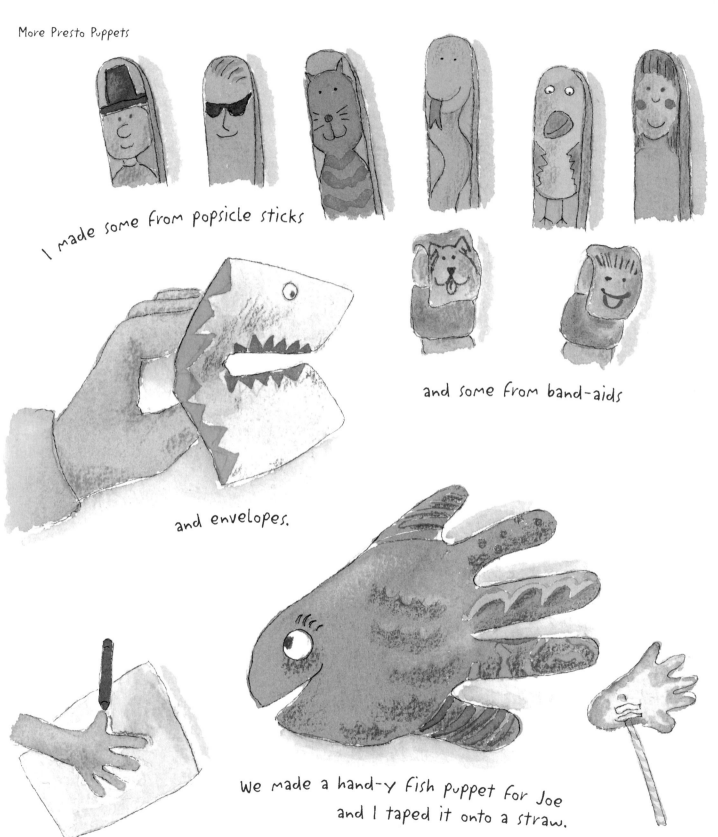

I made some from popsicle sticks

and envelopes.

and some from band-aids

We made a hand-y fish puppet for Joe
and I taped it onto a straw.

"These really are wonderful. I made some of these with my grandmother. I had forgotten all about them," said Grandma.

There was one kind of puppet I know Grandma never made and that's a soccer-playing puppet.

We drew soccer players. Mine looked just like me and had the same number I have.

YOU'LL NEED:
★ heavy paper
★ scissors
★ markers or crayons

Draw your puppet. Draw holes to fit your fingers.
  Cut out the figure. Cut out finger holes.
  Put your fingers through the holes and play ball!

It's easy if you fold back circles and cut out half moons.

We found a marble which we kicked with our fingers. We had a great game, until Grandma decided she could hardly wait for her hosts to serve lunch.

39

Fun and games

After our gala luncheon, Joe wasn't the only one ready for a nap. Grandpa said, "Isn't there a nice video you'd like to watch? Better yet, how 'bout a round of the quiet game? Whoever can keep quiet the longest wins!"

"No way," I said. "We're your entertainers and we're not going to let you down."

We got Grandpa's interest with a game called "Grandfather, May I?"

Grandfather, May I?

The player who's "Grandfather" stands on one side of the room, with the other players in a line on the opposite side.

"Grandfather" faces the players and, starting at one end of the line, gives each player a command. You can improvise, but some of the traditional commands are any number you choose of…giant steps, umbrella steps, ballerina steps, baby steps, frog hops…

The player can execute "Grandfather's" orders only if he asks "Grandfather, may I?" If he forgets his manners, he must go back to the starting line.

The first player whose good manners take him to "Grandfather" wins.

We twirled like umbrellas and hopped like frogs and did whatever Grandpa told us, until he told us to find a game with less hopping!

40

My Grandmother's Attic

The first player says, "In my grandmother's attic I found an..." and comes up with something that begins with "a".

The second player repeats the first object and adds one beginning with "b".

The next player repeats the first two objects and adds an item beginning with "c".

For instance, the fourth player says, "In my grandmother's attic I found an apple, a ballerina, a crayon, and a dog biscuit."

The game keeps going as long as all the players can remember what went before.

Then we played a game I knew Grandma would like, called "My Grandmother's Attic." Each player has to remember and repeat a whole long list of things.

"These games are a great way to improve your memory," Violet informed us.

"Let the games begin before I forget how to play!" laughed Grandma.

Grandma's always joking about how much she forgets, when she's really the best rememberer I know.

Cut-up Card Trick

YOU'LL NEED:
✦ a large index card or piece of paper about 5" by 8" (12 cm by 20 cm)
✦ scissors

Fold in half lengthwise. Make alternate cuts at about 1/2" (1.25 cm) intervals between the folded and the open end. Be sure to stop just before you reach each edge.

Also make sure that your first and last cuts start at the fold as shown.

Open the card and cut along the centerfold —leaving the strip on each end uncut.

Pull open and insert your body!

Before long, Joe was asleep on Grandma's lap.

"This is one laptop where I understand all the programs," she said.

Grandpa was dozing in the chair. I know from personal experience that a nap in the afternoon is deadly boring. I nudged Grandpa and asked him if he thought I could fit my whole body into a small card. He woke up immediately!

I showed him how I could fold a small card in half

so that when I cut along the centerfold

it opened into a card big enough for me to fit through.

42

Newspapers on parade

"Holy moly," said Grandpa, "I've never even looked at today's paper!"

Violet and I smiled at each other. Things really were going well.

Grandpa must not have been bored for one minute.

"Don't worry," I said, "your paper won't go to waste!"

I showed Grandpa how to make a great newspaper hat.

Sarah's Easy Paper Hat

YOU'LL NEED:
- ☆ a full sheet of newspaper

1. Fold the newspaper in half from left to right (along the fold).

2. Fold in half again from top to bottom.

3. Fold the top left until it meets the middle.

4. Repeat with the right so it looks like a house.

5. With the point away from you, fold the top two layers up to the roof line of the house.

6. Fold it one more time to look like a pant cuff.

7. Flip over and do the same two folds on the other side.

   Hold the bottom of the triangle and open up your new hat.

Tip: Staple, tape, or paper clip for a more stable hat.

Presto! I'd turned Grandpa's newspaper into a hat.

Grandpa showed me an even better one.

He measured out a square of newspaper. He had to do it very slowly so I could follow. After a lot of fancy fiddling and folding, he made an amazing Samurai hat.

"I hadn't thought about how to make that hat in years. But it all came back. Just like a fish riding a bicycle," he said, and he winked at Grandma.

Grandpa's Samurai Hat

YOU'LL NEED:
⭐ a full sheet of newspaper

Tip:

HOW TO MAKE A SQUARE:
Fold the upper corner of the paper until it meets the opposite edge. Cut off the excess from the bottom. Unfold to a perfect square.

Always fold along the dotted lines in the direction of the arrows.

1. Fold the square into a triangle with the fold along the top.

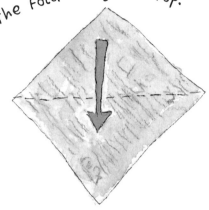

2. Fold the side flaps towards the center.

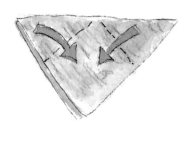

3. Fold the front layer of the bottom half up as shown.

4. To make the fancy horns fold the front layer of the top flaps out. Then fold up the front layer of the bottom half as shown.

5. Fold the bottom flap one more time to look like a pant cuff.

6. Fold the remaining layer of the bottom half up and into the hat. Staple, tape, or paper clip the corners.

45

We all made newspaper hats.

"All we need are a few instruments and we've got a parade!" I said.

So we banged wooden spoons on pots and pans and marched around the house. (Except Violet, who thought she was too old to bang on pots, so she banged on the piano instead.)

We marched and sang and danced around and sang and marched some more.

After we had done all there possibly was to do, it was almost time for Mom and Dad to come home. We asked Grandma and Grandpa how they liked being entertained.

"It's been the busiest two days of our lives," they said at the same time. "We weren't even a little bit bored— not for one minute."

We acknowledge the support of the Canada Council for the Arts, the Ontario Arts Council, and the Government of Canada through the Book Publishing Industry Development Program (BPIDP) for our publishing activities.

Cataloging in Publication Data

Hunter, Dette, 1943-
    38 ways to entertain your grandparents / by Dette Hunter ; art by Deirdre Betteridge.

ISBN 1-55037-749-3 (bound).—ISBN 1-55037-748-5 (pbk.)

    1. Indoor games—Juvenile literature. 2. Handicraft—Juvenile literature. 3. Cookery—Juvenile literature. 4. Grandparent and child—Juvenile literature. I. Betteridge, Deirdre II. Title.

TT160.H86 2002   j793   C2002-901276-7

The art in this book was rendered in watercolor.

Distributed in Canada by:
Firefly Books Ltd.
3680 Victoria Park Avenue
Willowdale, ON
M2H 3K1

Published in the U.S.A. by Annick Press (U.S.) Ltd.
Distributed in the U.S.A. by:
Firefly Books (U.S.) Inc.
P.O. Box 1338
Ellicott Station
Buffalo, NY 14205

Printed in Canada by Friesens, Altona, Manitoba

Acknowledgments
The idea for *Thirty-eight Ways to Entertain Your Grandparents* came from Sheryl Shapiro of Annick Press. The inspiration for the story came from my family and all the other wonderful grandparents and grandchildren I know. I thank them all. —*Dette Hunter*

visit us at: www.annickpress.com